Glimpses of Old
Newcastle

by Andrew Clark

An advert for the Newcastle upon Tyne Co-operative Society from 1939. It lists over 40 local branches and includes an illustration of their Central Premises in Newgate Street (see page 22).

Copyright Andrew Clark 2017

First published in 2017 by

Summerhill Books

PO Box 1210, Newcastle upon Tyne NE99 4AH

email: summerhillbooks@yahoo.co.uk

www.summerhillbooks.co.uk

ISBN: 978-1-911385-16-5

No part of this publication may be reproduced, stored in a mechanical retrieval system, or transmitted, in any form or by any means, electronic, mechanical, photocopying, recording or otherwise, without prior permission of the author.

Contents

Introduction	5
The Changing City Centre	6
Along The River	14
Newcastle at Work	18
The Co-op	22
Planes, Trains & Automobiles	24
Going to the Pictures	28
Tyne Tees Television	32
The North East Coast Exhibition	33
Last Orders For Old Pubs	34
Around Newcastle	38
Standing on the Terraces	44

Ice on the River Tyne around the Swing Bridge in 1963. The big freeze of that winter started in late December 1962 and lasted until the following March. The Swing Bridge is featured on page 15.

Looking down Pilgrim Street towards the Tyne Bridge around 1920. This photograph was taken at the junction with Worswick Street which can be seen on the left. The changes at the foot of Pilgrim Street in the 1960s are featured on page 11.

Bibliography and Further Reading

Benwell's Lost Coal Mines – Heritage Trail
by St James' Heritage & Environment Group, 2016

Cinemas of Newcastle
by Frank Manders, Newcastle City Library and Arts, 1991

Durham Coal – A People's History
by Andrew Clark & George Nairn, The People's History, 2001

Gateshead Remembered
by Anthea Lang, Summerhill Books, 2014

Heady Days – A History of Newcastle's Public Houses: Volume One the Central Area
by Brian Bennison, Newcastle City Library and Arts, 1996

Not Just Bricks and Mortar
by Jimmy Donald, Newcastle City Library and Arts, 1994

Westerhope Remembered
by Tom Peacock & Ron Handley, Summerhill Books, 2010

Co-operative Society Handbooks

Kelly's and Ward's Trade Directories

Kenton Local History Society Bulletin, 1990

River Tyne Official Handbook, 1925

Newspapers and Periodicals

Newcastle Journal   Evening Chronicle

Newcastle Courant   Sunderland Echo

Monthly Chronicle of North Country Lore and Legend

Introduction

'Glimpses of Old Newcastle' is a collection of picture postcards, archive photographs, adverts and memories that show how the city has changed over the years. Many of the postcards are from around a hundred years ago and it is interesting to compare the same scene today. There are a number of 'then and now' pages in the book with the modern photographs showing a very different Newcastle in 2017. Taking these 'now' pictures is often a hazardous task for the photographer. A hundred years ago you could take your time setting up your photograph in the middle of Grainger Street or Shields Road and not worry about cars or buses. Try doing that now with today's traffic!

We start our journey into Newcastle's past with the changing city centre with images that show the old streets, buildings, cafés, shops and markets. Then there is a trip along the riverside followed by photographs showing Newcastle at work. Favourite former cinemas and pubs are remembered before we finish on the terraces of St James' Park.

I have very much enjoyed working on this book and I would like thank everyone who has helped me.

Andrew Clark
Summerhill Books, 2017

Trolley buses outside the Central Station in the 1950s. A hundred years of developments at the Central Station can be seen on page 25.

Acknowledgements

Summerhill Books would like to thank the following people who have supplied photographs and memories for this book:

Derek Allan, Alan Brett, Philip Curtis, Ian Clough, Jack Hair, Ron Handley, Anthea Lang, Fred Millican, George Nairn, Tom Peacock, Sharyn Taylor, Mike Young and Yvonne Young

Beamish Museum, West Newcastle Picture History Collection

The Changing City Centre

Above: An aerial view of Newcastle city centre before the redevelopment of the 1960s and '70s. In the foreground, much of the area around old Eldon Square was demolished to make way for the indoor shopping centre of Eldon Square, opened in 1977.

Left: A closer view of Eldon Square around 1910. On the left is the east terrace – the only original side to remain after the west and north terraces were pulled down.

Left: Eldon Square in 2017. The war memorial, with the statue of St George slaying the dragon, was unveiled in 1923. The words 'Memory Lingers Here' are on the north side of the memorial.

A postcard view of Northumberland Street with cars, trams and horse and carts in the 1920s. The postcard was published by Robert Johnston of Gateshead and several of the photographs in this book were taken by him. On the far left is the horse-drawn London & North Eastern Railway's Express Parcels Service. Fenwick's department store, on the left, are advertising a sale – somethings do not change.

Northumberland Street in 2017. Today this street, like a number in Newcastle's city centre, is now pedestrianised and shoppers do not have to worry about cars – the days of trams and horse-drawn vehicles are long gone. Northumberland Street is still a popular shopping destination despite the modern trend for people to visit indoor malls and retail parks. Many household names occupy its shops.

The draper's shop of John James Fenwick in Northumberland Street in the early 1900s. The building had originally been built for a Doctor Baird in the 1820s and was acquired by Mr Fenwick sixty years later. His business was a great success and in 1913 neighbouring buildings were bought. The property was redeveloped into the very popular department store we know today.

Looking down Blackett Street at the junction of Northumberland Street around 1920. A tram and a couple of cars are driving towards where the photographer would be standing in the middle of the road. Do that now and you would soon be in trouble from the many buses that use this busy junction controlled by a set of traffic lights. In this photograph, almost a hundred years ago, a white gloved policeman is in charge of the traffic. Today there are a restrictions to the vehicles that can use this section of Blackett Street.

Left: A night time view of the Eldon Grill restaurant on the corner of Grey Street and Blackett Street in the 1930s. On the ground floor is one of a number of fruiters that Barry Noble had on Tyneside.

An advert for the Eldon Grill that appeared in a Theatre Royal programme in 1953 – '3 minutes from this Theatre.'

Left: A day time view of the Eldon Buildings in 2017. The Charles Grey public house now occupies the Eldon Grill while Berrys jewellers is in the shop on the ground floor.

Above: A 1948 advert for the Bairns' Shop that was on the second floor of John Moses drapers shop in Grainger Street – *Dainty Little Garments for Dainty Little People. The kiddies love being "Rigged Out" in the Storey-book surroundings of the "Bairns' Shop."*

Right: A view of Grainger Street and Grey's Monument in the 1940s. John Moses & Co Ltd can be glimpsed on the far left. Moses shop was in business in Grainger Street from the 1880s to around 1960.

A view of Grainger Street from the corner of the Bigg Market in the 1940s. On the left is one of a number of Carricks Restaurants that were in the city centre at the time – this one was called the 'Imperial'. Carricks also had the 'Dickens' in Grainger Street, the 'City' in Northumberland Street, the 'Cottage' in Northumberland Road as well as cafés at the Haymarket and Monument.

The Bigg Market and the Town Hall, looking from Grainger Street, in the 1920s. A tram on its way to the Monument has stopped to let passengers on and off. The Town Hall was demolished in 1973, after the Council services had moved to the Civic Centre at Barras Bridge in the late 1960s.

The corner of Neville Street and Grainger Street around 1910. A tram makes it way through what is now a pedestrian and cyclist area. On the right is the Douglas Hotel and opposite is another Barry Noble fruiters. Further up Grainger Street is St John the Baptist Church.

Collingwood Street around 1903. On the left, the Collingwood Buildings are in the process of being built. This corner had previously been the site of the Wellington pub. On the right is gun manufacturer W.R. Pape. This building was demolished a few years after this photograph was taken and the Sun Life offices built in its place.

Collingwood Street in 2017. The entrance to Revolutions bar is on the corner of the Collingwood Buildings. This had previously been Barclays Bank. To the far left student accommodation can be glimpsed. This has replaced the unpopular Westgate House that was demolished in 2007. The Sun Life Building on the right is now occupied by a number of other businesses.

Pilgrim Street in the 1930s. On the far left can just be seen a street sign for 'Low Bridge'. This lane ran to Dean Street. In 2017 there is still a sign for Low Bridge on Dean Street at the bottom of steps that lead to Pilgrim Street. In the 1960s this area was at the centre of massive redevelopment with the building of the Central Motorway and Swan House Roundabout.

Pilgrim Street in 2017. It was difficult to match exactly the scene above as doing so would have meant standing on the busy slip road that leads from the Tyne Bridge. The two buildings on the corner of Mosley Street remain, however, a number of buildings in the foreground have been replaced.

The construction of the roundabout and underpass at the foot of Pilgrim Street in the mid 1960s. Swan House was built in the middle of the roundabout and was for many years occupied by British Telecom.

The roundabout and the Central Motorway in 2017. The old Swan House, renamed 55 Degrees North in 2002, has been converted into apartments, restaurants and the home of Metro Radio.

The Vegetable Market on Newgate Street around 1910. The corner of Darn Crook (now St Andrew's Street) is bottom left. Many of the buildings in this photograph have now gone to be replaced by new shops, pubs and restaurants. One of the few buildings to survive is St Andrew's Church that can be glimpsed on the left.

Clayton Street from the junction of Newgate Street around 1920. Tram lines run up Clayton Street and a policeman controls the traffic to allow pedestrians to cross the cobbled road. On the left is Brooks which was advertising hats and caps with a display in their window – essential clothing for every man at that time.

The same view as above in 2017. Now cars and buses run down Clayton Street with a set of lights controlling the traffic. On the left is the former site of the Newgate Centre (a hotel and indoor shopping mall). The Newgate Centre stood here from the 1980s. It only survived thirty years while the surrounding buildings are over 150 years old.

The Cattle Market near to the Central Station in the early 1900s. The market survived until the 1960s.

The Cattle Market Keeper's House that still stands today in Times Square, surrounded by the Centre of Life. The building was designed by the great architect John Dobson in 1831. In this photograph from 1979 it was the home of a company selling garden sheds, garages and greenhouses.

Marlborough Crescent Bus Station in 1986. In the background is Anderson and Garland auction rooms, the Sun and News of the World office and Olley's Bar on the corner.

The Centre of Life and the entrance to Times Square in 2017. The bus station was demolished in the 1990s and the science village and visitor attraction the Centre for Life opened in 2000. Olley's Bar has had a name change to the Central – while a Persian restaurant occupies the newspaper building. A single bus stop is the only reminder of the old Marlborough Crescent Bus Station.

Along The River

A sketch of the quayside from 1880s. In the background is the High Level Bridge opened in 1849 and built for road and rail traffic. A docker rolls a barrel along and note the train lines that were once on the quayside. It would be forty years after this illustration was drawn that the Tyne Bridge was built.

A postcard titled 'The New Tyne Bridge (6th September 1928)'. This is one of a series of postcards showing the building of the bridge. There are cranes on the far left and work still has to be done on the towers on the Gateshead side. A month after this photograph was taken, the Tyne Bridge was officially opened by King George V and Queen Mary on 10th October 1928. The ship berthed by the quay is the *Sverdrup* from Bergen. Barrels are lined up for carts to take them away.

A much quieter scene in this photograph taken in 2017. Gone are the ships, their cargo and the many men who worked on the quayside. Now this area is used more for leisure and attracts visitors from not only this country but from around the world.

The open Swing Bridge allows the collier *Wychwood* to pass through – most likely to pick up a cargo of coal at Dunston Staithes. A crowd of people on the bridge watch the vessel come through. Built on the Wear in 1907, the *Wychwood* was in service for only ten years. The collier was sunk in 1917 by a German U-boat on its way to Scapa Flow to deliver coal to the Royal Navy. Three lives were lost.

Right: Ice on the River Tyne in the big freeze of 1963. The *Salvor* is berthed alongside the Swing Bridge.

The Swing Bridge was built in 1876, replacing the old stone bridge, allowing larger vessels access to the Tyne west of the city centre. In the years between the two World Wars over 10,000 ships a year passed through the bridge – on average at least three vessels a day.

Right: This view from 2017 shows the Swing Bridge's jetty that was surrounded by ice in the photograph above. It is no longer used and the small hut has disappeared. The Swing Bridge still operates over 140 years after it was first constructed. However, the days when it was open three times a day are long gone. Now it opens around four times a week. The Bridge is a popular local attraction and tours of its inner workings are well attended.

A view of the quayside from the early 1900s, taken from the Swing Bridge. At this time the quayside was a busy working environment with ships berthed every day. The buildings alongside the quay would be the offices of companies associated with shipping. Now most of these premises are occupied by restaurants, bars and cafés.

A hundred years later and the Tyne Bridge dominates the view of the quayside. A few boats are berthed at the quay but visitors today tend to be pleasure boats. In the distance is the latest bridge to span the Tyne – The Millennium Bridge. This section of the quayside is popular with walkers and cyclists with some on route to Cumbria if they are aiming to complete the Hadrian's Wall Path.

Right: A docker on the quayside tucks into his dinner while resting against a bollard in 1942. His food had come from the mobile British Restaurant behind him. British Restaurants were set up during the war to supply cheap meals to the public and at this time were serving over a half million meals a day.

Far right: One of the few remaining bollards on the quayside in 2017. In the background are the Swing Bridge and the High Level Bridge.

The Redheugh Bridge in the early 1900s, shortly after it was opened in 1901. This was the second crossing at Redheugh. The first bridge had been built in 1871 and survived for thirty years. The bridge shown on the right had a longer life-span of eighty years before it was replaced.

All that remains of the old Redheugh Bridge are the abutments on the Gateshead side – seen on the right with the present bridge alongside it. This third Redheugh crossing was opened in 1983 by Princess Diana and was built to last over 100 years. The artwork on the wall of the old abutments is a steel sculpture called 'Once Upon a Time' by Turner Prize winning artist Richard Deacon, installed in 1990.

The old Scotswood Bridge known as the 'Chain Bridge'. Opened in 1831, the bridge was immortalised in the song 'Blaydon Races' by Geordie Ridley:

We flew across the Chain Bridge reet into Blaydon Toon,

The bellman he was callin' there, they call him Jackie Broon;

Aa saw him talkin' to sum cheps, an' them he was persuadin'

To gan an' see Geordie Ridley's concert in the Mechanics' Hall at Blaydon.

The Chain Bridge survived for over 130 years before a new crossing at Scotswood was built in the mid 1960s. The new bridge was constructed alongside the old and can be seen nearing completion in the photograph on the left in 1967. A small sign in the foreground points the way to Blaydon. After the present bridge was opened in March of that year, the Chain Bridge was demolished.

Newcastle at Work

The Durham and Northumberland Collieries Fire and Rescue Brigade that was based on the corner of Scotswood Road and Hannah Street in 1912. At this time there were collieries in Scotswood (Montagu Pit), Benwell (Beaumont, Charlotte and Edward Pits), Elswick, Walker, West Denton, Walbottle and Throckley.

A brochure produced by the Rescue Service described its early history:

'In 1910 a Rescue Committee was formed by the Durham and Northumberland Coal Owners' Association under the Chairmanship of Colonel W.C. Blackett, and a Rescue Station was erected at Elswick, Newcastle upon Tyne. Mr Guy Symond, Chief Officer of the Works Fire Brigade of Sir W.G. Armstrong Whitworth & Co Ltd, was appointed in charge of the Brigade with a permanent staff of men. Recognising early that fire would probably require more serious consideration than would be the results of explosions, the colliery owners determined not only to have men trained in the use of breathing apparatus, but also to have them skilled to fight fires. A motor engine and a motor rescue tender were provided and equipped for emergencies of fire and explosion at mines. In 1911 the Coal Mines' Act was passed with Regulations which made it the duty of the Coal Owners to make adequate provision for the establishment of Central Rescue Stations and for the maintenance of rescue appliances within every 10 miles radius of coal mines.'

A badge of the Durham and Northumberland Collieries Fire and Rescue Brigade.

After the coal industry was nationalised in 1947 the NCB's Regional Fire and Rescue Service was based at Benwell Towers (*left*) until 1976. The Towers later became a pub called the Mitre and then home to the TV series 'Byker Grove'. It is now an Islamic School.

The launch of the HMS *Invincible* from Armstrong's Elswick shipyard on the 18th April 1907. The vessel took part in a number of battles in the First World War before being sunk on 31st May 1916. W.G. Armstrong started his works at Elswick (*right*) in 1847 and manufactured hydraulic machinery and armaments. Shipbuilding was started at Elswick in the 1880s. As the First World War approached Armstrong's established

the Naval Yard at Walker and by 1915 employed 3,500 men. In the 1920s Armstrong's merged with Vickers to become one of the major warship manufactures in the world. During the Second World War dozens of ships were built at the Naval Yard.

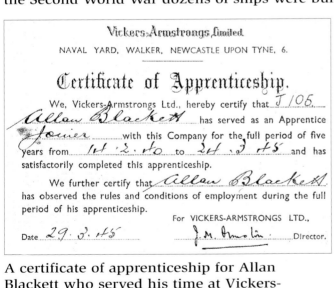

A certificate of apprenticeship for Allan Blackett who served his time at Vickers-Armstrong's Naval Yard, Walker in the 1940s.

In 1968 the Naval Yard became part of the Swan Hunter's group. HMS *Ark Royal* was built at Swan's and launched in 1981. The aircraft carrier was fitted out at the Naval Yard and when work was completed the yard was closed.

Right: An advert for Vickers – 'A famous name on Tyneside' – from the 1960s.

Above: Kenton Quarries in the early 1900s. Note the number of circular millstones stacked up. In 1939 the quarry was advertising stone for the 'Garden Beautiful' that included natural crazy paving, bird baths, sundials and 'coarse Kenton stone specially selected for rockeries'.

Right: There is millstone alongside the old windmill at Cowgate in an illustration from around 1900. Next door is the Windmill pub that was rebuilt in the 1930s before being demolished in the 1990s.

More hard work from the early 1900s – this time a group of men take a break to have their photograph taken alongside their steam roller. It was owned by Gosforth road contractor William Bland. The name of the engine was 'Dora' – perhaps named after a relative of Mr Bland.

Right: Inside Maling's Ford Pottery in the early 1900s. The firm moved to Newcastle in 1817 and by 1900 the company employed over 1,000 workers producing one and a half million items a month. The majority of its workforce were women. The Hoult family bought the firm after the Second World War but the pottery would only last to 1963. The Ford Pottery site is now known as Hoults Yard.

Below: An advert for Maling Ware from 1929.

Workers at the Adamsez factory around 1916. The firm was founded by twin brothers called Adams and they manufactured sanitary ware at their Scotswood factory. This photograph, taken during the First World War, shows one man in uniform in the back row. Perhaps he was visiting the works that day. Production at Scotswood ended in the 1970s.

The former Robert Sinclair Tobacco premises on St James Boulevard in 2017.

Left: A group of women workers at the Robert Sinclair factory during the Second World War. One man joins them for this photograph.

The Co-op

Right: A sketch from the 1890s of the Newcastle upon Tyne Co-operative Society's Central Stores in Newgate Street. This was the Co-op's first main premises in Newcastle. It was replaced in the 1930s by the art deco building that still stands today.

The Co-operative Movement owes its formation to a group in Rochdale in 1844. The aim of these 'Rochdale Pioneers' was to sell 'honest food at honest prices'. Co-operatives quickly spread throughout the country.

Left: A group of men going on a trip in a Newcastle Co-operative Society vehicle around 1920. They are outside the old Newgate Street premises and behind them is the sign for the Juvenile Youth and Mens Clothing Department.

The Society's new Central Premises (*below*) was open from 1932 until 2011, although in its last four years only the food hall on the ground floor was operating.

Right: An advert from 1953 promoting the travel department in the Co-op's Newgate Street Central Store.

As well as their main premises, the Co-operative had over 40 local branches in Newcastle as well stores in Ponteland and Hazlerigg. An advert from 1948 described the Co-op as 'The Family Store' and that there is 'A Branch Near Every Home'.

The former Co-op Store in Newgate Street was converted into restaurants and a hotel that opened in 2016.

On the corner of Bath Lane and Rutherford Street stands the former building of the Newcastle Branch of the Co-operative Printing Society. The illustration on the right shows the newly-opened printers in the 1890s. A Co-op Handbook gave this description of the interior: 'The building will be lined throughout with cream-coloured glazed bricks, which besides giving a very cheerful aspect to the workshops, saves the cost and trouble of annual whitewashing.' The photograph above far right shows the building in 2017. It is now occupied by a Japanese Restaurant and the Danish electrical dealer Bang & Olufsen.

An illustration showing two Co-operative Wholesale Society buildings in Newcastle in the 1890s. On the left is the Thornton Street warehouse that housed the furnishing and provision departments. On the right is part of the Waterloo Street building that contained the drapery department.

The two buildings above survived until the 1970s when they were demolished and the flats of Thornton Court were built on the site (*left*).

The Co-op owned a number of other properties in Newcastle that still stand today. In Waterloo Street is Arthur Wilson House. In the 1970s this building was converted into a cinema, then later a nightclub and is now apartments. There is also the former banana ripening warehouses in Stowell Street. The Discovery Museum in Blandford Square was a former Co-operative Wholesale Society warehouse as was the Malmaison Hotel on the quayside.

Planes, Trains & Automobiles

Right: Two photographs of the terminal buildings of Woolsington Airport in the 1950s. Some of these were former RAF huts from the Second World War.

In the late 1950s there were around 42,000 passengers using the airport – within ten years it had increased to nearly 200,000. The 1960s saw more people travelling abroad for their holidays and the airport's capacity struggled to meet these needs. A £1.8 million development completed in 1966 improved the terminal buildings, walkways and provided restaurants, bars and shops. The runways were extended but before this was done 18th century mine workings were opened and filled in to prevent subsidence.

In the 1970s Woolsington Airport was renamed Newcastle Airport.

The airport after expansion in the mid 1960s. Prime Minister Harold Wilson officially opened the terminal building in February 1967. For the next fifty years Newcastle International Airport has continued to expand and in 2015 celebrated its 80th anniversary. The following year 4.8 million passengers used the airport.

An illustration of the Central Station and Neville Street from 1889. The station was built for £90,000 and opened by Queen Victoria in 1850. A number of horse-drawn trams and cabs can be seen. In the late 19th century the cab fare from the Central Station to a city centre hotel was a shilling.

The Central Station and Neville Street around 1914. Electric trams have replaced the horse-drawn vehicles of the above illustration. Electric lighting was introduced in the station in 1900 and four years later electric trains started running.

The Central Station and Neville Street in 2017. A major renovation of the station and surrounding area was started in 2013 costing £20 million. This included glazing over the arches of the portico seen in the centre of the photograph. Bus stops now line Neville Street.

Tram number 191 to Newburn stops below a low bridge around 1910. The tram's conductor and driver pose for the photographer as do some of the passengers on the top deck.

A sign on the bridge advises: 'Car passengers must not stand when passing under Bridge. It is DANGEROUS to touch the Wires.'

Two 'Ha'penny Lops' in the early 1900s. These were horse brakes with a halfpenny fare that operated between Newcastle and Gateshead using the High Level Bridge (seen far right). Trams did not run over the bridge until it was strengthened in 1923 and so brakes, that could carry up to 40 passengers, provided a horse-drawn service.

A conductor stands by this Newcastle Corporation trolley bus in St Nicholas Street in the 1930s. This is now a one-way street and the trolley bus and cars would be facing the wrong way today. Trolley buses continued to run in Newcastle up to 1966, sixteen years after the Corporation stopped running trams. In 1980 a new form of electric-powered public transport was opened on Tyneside – the Metro.

The bus that ran from Stanley to Newcastle before the Second World War. Stanley historian Jack Hair recalled as a boy in the 1940s travelling on a similar bus on a visit to Newcastle. On his way home he and his grandmother had to get off the bus and walk behind it as the vehicle struggled up the steep hills on the journey to Stanley.

A bus passes the Jingling Gate pub at Westerhope before the First World War. A regular service had started in 1912 that ran from Whorlton though Westerhope and on to Newcastle, terminating at Fenham Barracks. At this time any workmen coming from work in their dirty clothes were only allowed to use the top deck. It must have been a cold ride on the open top deck where the conductor is standing.

Customers from the Black Bull pub on Barrack Road are about to set off to support Newcastle United at Wembley for the FA Cup Final. Ian Clough who supplied the photograph gives this description of the fans: 'James Irwin President/Secretary of Newcastle Supporters' Club and Manager of the Black Bull sits with a back seat full of beer and cigarettes while six of the Wembley-bound supporters (and dog) take a photo call.'

Going to the Pictures

Here in Pilgrim Street in the 1960s we see three examples of Newcastle's past – the Odeon Cinema with a Newcastle Transport bus outside advertising Newcastle Ales. The Odeon (then called the Paramount) was opened in 1931 and was one of the most popular picture houses in the city. After closing in 2002 the building stood empty until demolition started in January 2017 as this part of Pilgrim Street is being redeveloped.

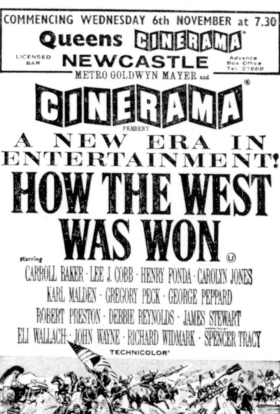

The Grainger Picture House before the Second World War. Known for showing the same film for week after week if popular, adverts would say 'retained next week'. The Grainger closed in 1960.

An advert for 'How The West Was Won' from October 1963. The Queens in Northumberland Place was known for showing the 'epic' films that were released in the 1950s and '60s. To compete with television, new ways of presenting films were introduced such as VistaVision, CinemaScope and 3-D. 'How The West Was Won' was shown in Cinerama – a projecting process using three screens. The Queens was closed in 1980 and the building was demolished.

Right: An advert for 'The Gold Rush' at the Grainger in 1956. Remembered for the scene where a hungry Charlie Chaplin eats his shoe, it was originally made as a silent in 1925. The film was re-issued in 1942 with sound effects and a narration from Chaplin.

```
GRAINGER
Retained Sunday and Next Week
     CHARLES CHAPLIN
   THE GOLD RUSH (u)
   At 1.15, 3.50, 6.25, 9.0.
```

The 02 Academy on the corner of Westgate Road and Clayton Street in 2017. This successful music venue was formerly the Gaumont cinema (previously the Westgate) and was showing films until the late 1950s. It was converted into a ballroom for a short time before turning to bingo for many years. The Gaumont was one four cinemas on a short stretch of Westgate Road. The other three were the Essoldo, the Stoll and the Pavilion.

An advert for 'Ben Hur' at the Essoldo in 1960. This biblical epic starring Charlton Heston is famous for its exciting chariot race. Prices for the film started at four shillings in the stalls to 10/6 for the best seats in the circle. The Essoldo cinema was open for over 50 years before being closed in 1990. Apartments now stand on the site.

The Stoll cinema in the early 1970s shortly before it closed in 1974. Opening in 1867 as the Tyne Theatre and Opera House, the popularity of films in the 20th century saw it converted into a cinema after the First World War by Sir Oswald Stoll. The Stoll was the first cinema in Newcastle to show talkies. On the side of the building can just be seen the word 'Talkies' to advertise the latest in film technology in the 1920s. Re-opening as a theatre in 1977, for forty years the theatre has hosted a variety of performances from comedy to ballet. In August 2017 films were once again shown as part of the Whitley Bay Film Festival.

The block of flats that was built on the site of another former cinema in Westgate Road – The Pavilion that was closed in 1975.

Scotswood Road with the Crown Picture House in the background in 1962. This photograph was taken on the day of the 100th anniversary of the Blaydon Races and the old car in the foreground was part of a procession of floats and other vehicles. The Crown cinema was closed later that year.

The Heaton Electric Cinema on Heaton Road was closed in 1961. After many years as a bingo hall, the building is now home to a church.

The Plaza on Westgate Road was closed in 1960 and like many former cinemas was converted into a bingo hall. It has stood empty for a number of years.

Before television became popular going to the pictures a couple of times a week was common. There were cinemas in most parts of Newcastle right up until the 1960s when many started to be turned into bingo halls. Young 'uns would look forward to the Saturday matinees while courting couples would book the double seats in the back row.

One lady from Whickham Local History Society recalls the time she had a new boyfriend from Newcastle and they went to the pictures together: 'All of my friends had partners and one Friday night we all booked the back row at our local cinema. I wanted to introduce my new boyfriend to my friends and it was the first time he had come to Whickham. So we are all sitting paired up in the double seats with no arm rests. Me and my fella were sharing an ice cream and he thought it was just for the two of us. Well, this ice cream was passed all the way along our row of seats and all my friends and their lads had a lick! That was the last time I saw my boyfriend. This sort of behaviour might have been acceptable in our village of Whickham but it wasn't the done thing in Newcastle.'

Left: An advert for Hinge's Circuit of local cinemas from 1954. The Regal on Two Ball Lonnen is now shops, beauty room and a snooker hall (*above in 2017*) while the Globe on Salters Road, Gosforth, is now a restaurant, interiors shop and beauty salon (*below in 2017*).

A postcard titled 'Mechanics Institute, Walker' from the 1920s. Another postcard by Robert Johnston of Gateshead. Above the door can just be seen the name 'Walker Picture House'. The Institute was the home of the cinema until a fire destroyed the building in 1949.

Tyne Tees Television

The Tyne Tees Television studios on City Road in the 1980s. Tyne Tees, the independent television channel for the North East, was launched in 1959. At that time television sets were available for rental from around 14 shillings a week.

In the early 1980s the building was extended to accommodate a new studio. Access to this studio was through a covered walkway known as the Tube which gave its name to one of the company's most famous programmes – the award-winning music show 'The Tube' that was broadcast on Channel 4 from 1982 to 87.

In 2005 Tyne Tees moved to new studios near the MetroCentre. Five years later the City Road buildings and the adjacent pub, the Egypt Cottage, were demolished.

An advert for Tyne Tees Television from 1962. The advert gave this description of the company: 'From the day it started transmissions in 1959, Tyne Tees Television has deliberately aimed at being the North East's own station by developing programmes of local interest coupled with a very high standard of production. Tyne Tees Television now has a loyal and enthusiastic audience of over two million viewers.'

Flats now stand on the part of the site of the former Tyne Tees Television studios on City Road.

On the fence of the apartment block is a series of artwork called 'End of Broadcast'. The colour design is based on the 'test screen', that was used in the 1980s, to commemorate the history of broadcasting in that area.

The North East Coast Exhibition

The Palace of Industry at the North East Coast Exhibition in 1929. The Exhibition was opened on 14th May by the Prince of Wales (later Edward VIII) as a showcase for local industry, crafts and business. Other buildings included the Palace of Engineering, the Palace of Arts, Festival Hall and Garden Club. The Exhibition ran until 26th October 1929 and by then there had been over four million visitors.

After the Exhibition closed the majority of the buildings were demolished but the Palace of Arts (*right*) survives to this day. For many years the building was used as a Science Museum and its most famous exhibit was the *Turbinia* – the world's first steam turbine-powered vessel built by Charles Parsons at Wallsend in 1894. The *Turbinia* is now housed on the ground floor in the Discovery Museum.

From 1983 to 2006 the former Palace of Arts was occupied by the Newcastle Military Vehicle Museum. After standing empty for ten years, the iconic building is now the home of Wylam Brewery. Events such as live music, comedy clubs, beer festivals and weddings are held in the Palace of Arts' Grand Hall.

One of the many attractions at the North East Coast Exhibition in 1929 was this giant ride called the Himalayan Railway.

Last Orders For Old Pubs

The Ye Olde Fighting Cocks in Albion Row, off Walker Road, in the 1960s. The pub was originally called the Fighting Cocks but 'Ye Olde' was added at one time. There is an advert on the side of the building for McEwan's Export: 'The Best Buy in Beer'.

William McEwan started brewing beer in Edinburgh in 1856. His firm later merged with another Scottish brewer William Younger. A further merger took place in 1960 with Newcastle Breweries to form Scottish & Newcastle. At this time the company's top three brands were McEwan's Export, Younger's Tartan Special and Newcastle Brown Ale.

Left: The former Fighting Cocks in 2017. The old pub has been converted into offices with an extension at the back. Newcastle has seen many pubs close over the years, however, a number of the buildings still survive and are now shops, restaurants, offices or flats.

An advert for the Cattle Market Inn and Commercial Hotel, Clayton Street West, from the 1870s. The advert claims: 'Quality, well aired beds'. In the late 19th century the average price for bed and breakfast in Newcastle hotels was five shillings.

The former Cattle Market Inn and Commercial Hotel in 2017. Now it is office premises. The pub was renamed the Market Commercial Inn and survived until the mid 1960s.

The old Rock Hotel that stood on the corner of Park Road and Cambridge Street, Elswick, between the late 19th century to the 1950s when it was rebuilt.

The Ye Old Brass Man pub that stood in Collingwood Street. At this time it was one of Robert Deuchar's pubs whose name dwarfs the size of the pub sign.

The rebuilt Rock Hotel in the 1960s. Behind the pub is a crane working on the tower block that was being built on Westmorland Road at that time.

The pub now named the Brass Man. Deuchars was taken over by Newcastle Breweries in the 1950s and their blue star hangs outside. The pub was closed in the early 1970s and demolished with a new building built on the site (*below*).

In 2017 the former pub is now flats and a convenience store. However, the Rock's signs still remain. In the background is Cruddas Park House.

The Sporting Arms on Denton Road in the 1960s. On the left is the office of the local Labour Party.

After being a pub for a century, the Sporting Arms was converted into a restaurant. The Labour Party office has now gone.

The Bay Horse Inn on Westgate Road in the 1960s.

In 2017 the former pub is occupied by a shop selling leather wear.

The Blue Bell Hotel on Shields Road, Byker in the 1960s. A sign on the pub points the way to Brough Park Stadium, the home of speedway and greyhound racing still open today.

The Blue Bell Hotel called last orders for the final time in the 1990s and the building is now the premises of the Edinburgh Bicycle Co-operative.

Percy Street around 1900. The tall building centre right is the then newly-built offices of Newcastle Breweries. Today, the brewery is long gone but this building is still standing and can be seen in the photograph below right in 2017. Now known as the Bruce Building, in 2015 it was redeveloped into apartments and offices. Before that, from the 1950s, it had been owned by King's College then Newcastle University.

The Newcastle Breweries Ltd name can still be seen above the main door (*above*) on Percy Street and on floor tiles on the inside of this door (*below*).

Newcastle Breweries was formed in 1890 when five local companies merged. One of those companies, John Barras, had its brewery in Bath Lane and this was to become the headquarters of Newcastle Breweries. Decades of expansion and mergers followed that saw the Tyne Brewery dominate this part of Newcastle. After the closure of the brewery in 2005 the majority of the buildings were demolished and new developments have taken their place. One of the few buildings to survive is the old administration office (*left*) that is now the Sandman Hotel overlooking St James' Park. On the side of the hotel is an old reminder of its former past – the Blue Star on the top right hand corner. This was the symbol of Newcastle Breweries with the five pointed star representing the five original companies.

Around Newcastle

Scotswood Road, looking west, around 1910. At this time the road was bustling with shops and pubs that were said to be on every corner. Today this road is a shadow of its former self with everything being swept away in the latter half of the 20th century.

Elswick Road looking towards Westgate Road in the early 1900s. In the distance, on the corner of Westgate Road, is the Robert Deuchar pub the Bay Horse. Deuchar's had many pubs on Tyneside at this time as well as their main offices on Sandyford Road. The Bay Horse was rebuilt after the Second World War and can be seen on page 36, when it was a Scottish & Newcastle pub. Opposite the Bay Horse, the tall building is the Westgate Mission Hall, built 1900-02.

Elswick Road in 2017. The Bay Horse is no longer a pub and is now a leather wear shop. On the far right, there is a general dealers on the corner where a pharmacists was a hundred years ago.

Above: Cows on the line! Leaves on the line may be a modern problem for today's trains, however, a hundred years ago these cows stopped this tram in Fenham. The conductor at the back of the tram is keeping an eye on this unusual hold up.

Right: A very peaceful scene in Wingrove Road a hundred years ago. This road runs from Westgate Road to Fenham Hall Drive.

Right: Wingrove Road now packed with parked cars on both sides in 2017. The girls with their bikes in the picture above would struggle to stand in the road to have their photograph taken today

West Avenue in Westerhope in the early 1900s. Beaumont Terrace is on the far left. The only people in sight are two young girls with a pushchair standing in the middle of the road. West Avenue was known locally as 'Clarty Avenue' – for obvious reasons. There is no traffic but the wheels of some carts have left their mark in the clarts.

A view of West Avenue in 2017. The clarts have been replaced by tarmac and the cart tracks by white lines for the many cars that now use this street. There are so many cars that traffic calming measures have had to be introduced – roughly where the two girls are standing in the photograph above.

The Walbottle Branch of the Throckley District Co-operative around 1900. On the right of the building was the drapery department while the grocery department was in the middle.

In 2017 the building is still in use but no longer by the Co-op. The ground floor is now occupied by a ladies hairdressers, traditional barbers, a fancy dress store and a restaurant, with a gym on the first floor.

Two postcards of Kenton Village from around the time of the First World War. They show a very rural scene and a quiet road with only a horse and cart in the photograph above while on the right three lads on bikes cycle through the village. On the far right is the Methodist Chapel which, along with many of the houses, was gone by the 1950s.

In this photograph taken in 2017 most of Kenton Village has disappeared. The only houses that remain are called Manor Farm Cottages. The traffic island in the foreground is handy for pedestrians trying to cross what can be a busy road near Kenton School.

A very old postcard of Heaton Park from the late 19th century. Two men are playing croquet in front of the Pavilion built in the 1880s. The croquet lawn was later turned into a bowling green that was popular well into the 21st century. The green is now no longer used. The Pavilion however is thriving and is the home of a restaurant.

Heaton Road looking towards Shields Road in the early part of the 20th century. On the right is the Heaton Branch of the Newcastle upon Tyne Co-operative Society. On the same side, further down, is the Presbyterian Church. On the left hand side of Heaton Road the local shops look very neat with their awnings.

Heaton Road in 2017. There are still the old signs for the Newcastle upon Tyne Co-operative Society on the building on the right but it is now occupied by a number of shops and business. The Presbyterian Church has gone and replaced with flats, although the church hall (just past the former Co-op building) remains.

Shields Road in Byker in the early 1900s. For many years Shields Road was a very popular area for shoppers and two of the favourite shops were Beavan's and Parrish's.

On the corner of Shields Road and Heaton Park Road once stood Beavan's drapery. The High Main pub now stands on this corner.

In 1910 a larger Beavan's store was built on Shields Road that still stands today. Although no longer called Beavan's and occupied by a number of shops, the old name can be seen on the building.

The other great former department store that once attracted shoppers from throughout Tyneside to Shields Road was Parrish's – seen above in 2017. Now the upper floors are flats while the retail units on the ground floor currently stand empty.

An advert from Parrish's in its heyday from 1939. Their slogan was: 'Come East! – Pay Least!'

Standing on the Terraces

Charlie Crowe scores the first goal against Portsmouth at St James' Park in 1956. Crowe's shot eluded both the Pompey goalkeeper, Norman Uprichard, and number nine Vic Keeble to find the net. Newcastle won the game 2-1 with a further goal from Harry Taylor. Charlie Crowe won a FA Cup Final medal at Wembley in 1951 and stayed at Newcastle for over ten years. Many years after retiring he shared his memories of United in two books 'Crowe Amongst The Magpies' and 'Charlie Crowe's Newcastle Scrapbook' that were sold to help raise £1.5 million for a medical scanner for Newcastle University.

The crowd at this match over sixty years ago is very different from today. Most of the fans are standing on the terraces with only those in the Main Stand having a seat – unlike today's all-seater stadium. However, there are plenty of lads sitting by the pitch. Many of these young 'uns would have been lifted up and passed over the heads of the crowd towards the front so they could have a clear view of the game. Westerhope historian Tom Peacock remembers going to St James' as a lad and he called being picked up like this as a 'spuggy's lift'.

The game was played in August but by the look of the supporters it must have been raining that day. Almost everyone is wearing a top coat while the few women in the crowd have head scarves on and one man at the back is sheltering under an umbrella.

There are no replica shirts, very few scarves but plenty of flat caps!

Left: The programme for Newcastle's home game against Blackpool on 25th April 1955. The United team that day included Jackie Milburn, Bob Stokoe, Jimmy Scoular and Ronnie Simpson in goal. Blackpool were one of the top sides in the country at that time and the game ended 1-1.

Wor Jackie Milburn takes on Everton right back Moore at St James' Park. Newcastle's most famous player of the 1950s was born in Ashington in 1924 and made his first team debut in the FA Cup in 1946. Jackie scored 177 goals for United and played in their three FA Cup finals at Wembley – 1951, '52 and '55.

Right: 'The Boot that Jack built' – an advert for Jackie Milburn's 'streamlined lightweight' football boots. The prices were 63 shillings for adults, with youth sizes 42 shillings and boys sizes 37/6d. The advert boasts: 'Many famous players say they are as "comfortable as a pair of gloves." The leather is selected by Milburn.'

The Jackie Milburn statue outside of St James' Park in 2017.

Celebrations in the Main Stand at St James' Park as Newcastle United bring home the Inter-Cities Fairs' Cup in 1969. The trophy is held aloft for the cheering crowd on the pitch. United had beaten the Hungarian side Ujpest Dozsa 6-2 on aggregate in a two-legged final. Captain Bob Moncur had scored two goals in the home tie and one away – his only ever goals for Newcastle. On the way to the final, United beat Feyenoord, Sporting Lisbon, Real Zaragoza, Vitoria Setubal and Glasgow Rangers. In the 1960s European football was still new to many fans and Newcastle became the first North East club to face foreign sides in competition. Fans, who are old enough to remember, have fond memories of these glory nights in Europe and of the last major trophy won by the Magpies.

The Fairs' Cup-winning side makes its way through the streets of Newcastle to St James' Park in 1969 in this advert for Armstrong Coaches.

Wyn 'The Leap' Davies challenges the Rangers' goalkeeper during the Fairs' Cup semi-final at Ibrox.

Right: St James Park in the 1960s. Two sides of the stadium do not have a roof and only the Main Stand had seats.

Newcastle supporter Evan Martin shares his memories of going to St James' Park from the 1950s: 'We started by standing in the Leazes End, then we started going in the Popular Side – now the East Stand. In the winter, the pitch was covered in straw to protect it from the bad weather. Newcastle always seemed to wait for the snow to fall and then put the straw over the pitch. They never went in for weather forecasts. Supporters would volunteer to clear snow or straw from the pitch. Often in the winter when I was a lad I would watch the game sitting in the straw around the pitch. It stunk! I didn't go in the paddocks until I was in my twenties – until I could afford it. Then I got a season ticket in the paddocks.'

Right: A model of the planned redevelopment of St James' Park from the early 1970s. The East Stand was built, however, it would be a further two decades before the Leazes End was improved.

In 1987 the Main Stand was pulled down to be replaced by the Milburn Stand. Further expansion continued throughout the 1990s with new all-seater stands at the Leazes and Gallowgate Ends. Further building work completed in 2000 saw the ground's capacity increased to over 52,000.

Right: St James' Park in the 21st century looking towards the Gallowgate End.

Also available from Summerhill Books

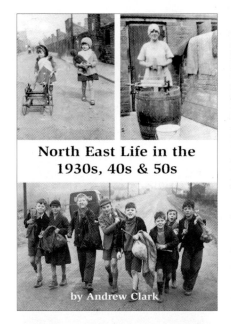
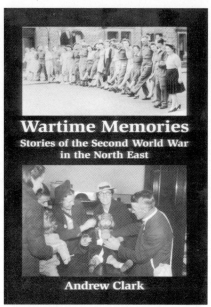
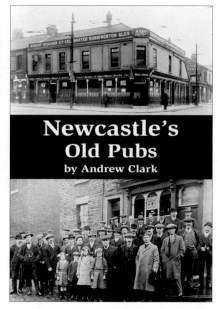
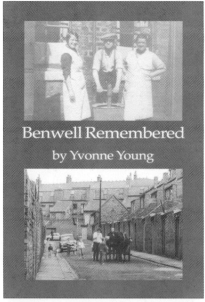
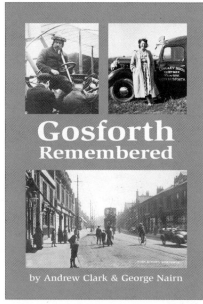
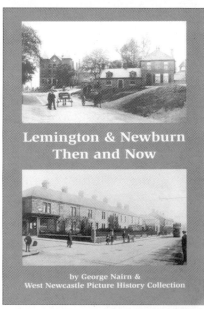
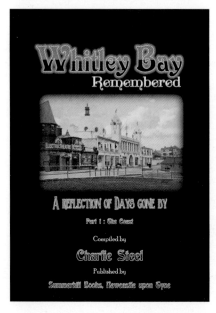
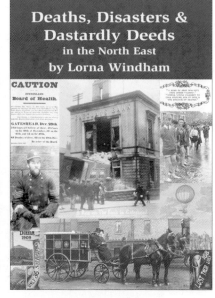
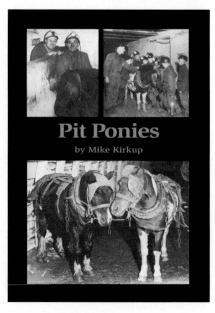

visit our website to view our full range of books
www.summerhillbooks.co.uk